Amazing Apes

by
David Orme

Thunderbolts

Amazing Apes
by David Orme

Illustrated by Dan Chernett

Published by Ransom Publishing Ltd.
Radley House, 8 St. Cross Road, Winchester, Hants. SO23 9HX, UK
www.ransom.co.uk

ISBN   978 178127 068 4
First published in 2013
Copyright © 2013 Ransom Publishing Ltd.

Illustrations copyright © 2013 Dan Chernett
'Get the Facts' section - images copyright: cover, prelims, passim – David Arvidsson, Thomas Lersch; pp 4/5 - Nino Verde; pp 6/7 - Delphine Bruyere, Ikiwaner, Kabir Bakie; pp 8/9 - David Arvidsson, Oliver Spalt; pp 10/11 - Dave Proffer, Mantis21, Sage Ross; pp 12/13 - Robert Churchill, Anna Zielińska, David Benbennick; pp 14/15 - Mike R, Breuer T, Ndoundou-Hockemba M, Fishlock V; pp 16/17 - Willie B. Thomas, efesan, Kabir Bakie; pp 18/19 - NASA; pp 20/21 - Andrzej Barabasz, MissHibiscus; pp 22/23 - photosmile2010, Boris Diakovsky, Marcus Lindström; p 36 - Joy Fera.

A CIP catalogue record of this book is available from the British Library.

All rights reserved. No part of this publication may be reproduced, stored in a retrieval system, or transmitted, in any form or by any means, electronic, mechanical, photocopying, recording or otherwise, without the prior permission of the publishers.

The rights of David Orme to be identified as the author and of Dan Chernett to be identified as the illustrator of this Work have been asserted by them in accordance with sections 77 and 78 of the Copyright, Design and Patents Act 1988.

Contents

Amazing Apes: The Facts — 5

The Burglars — 25

Amazing Apes: The Facts

Chimps and bonobos

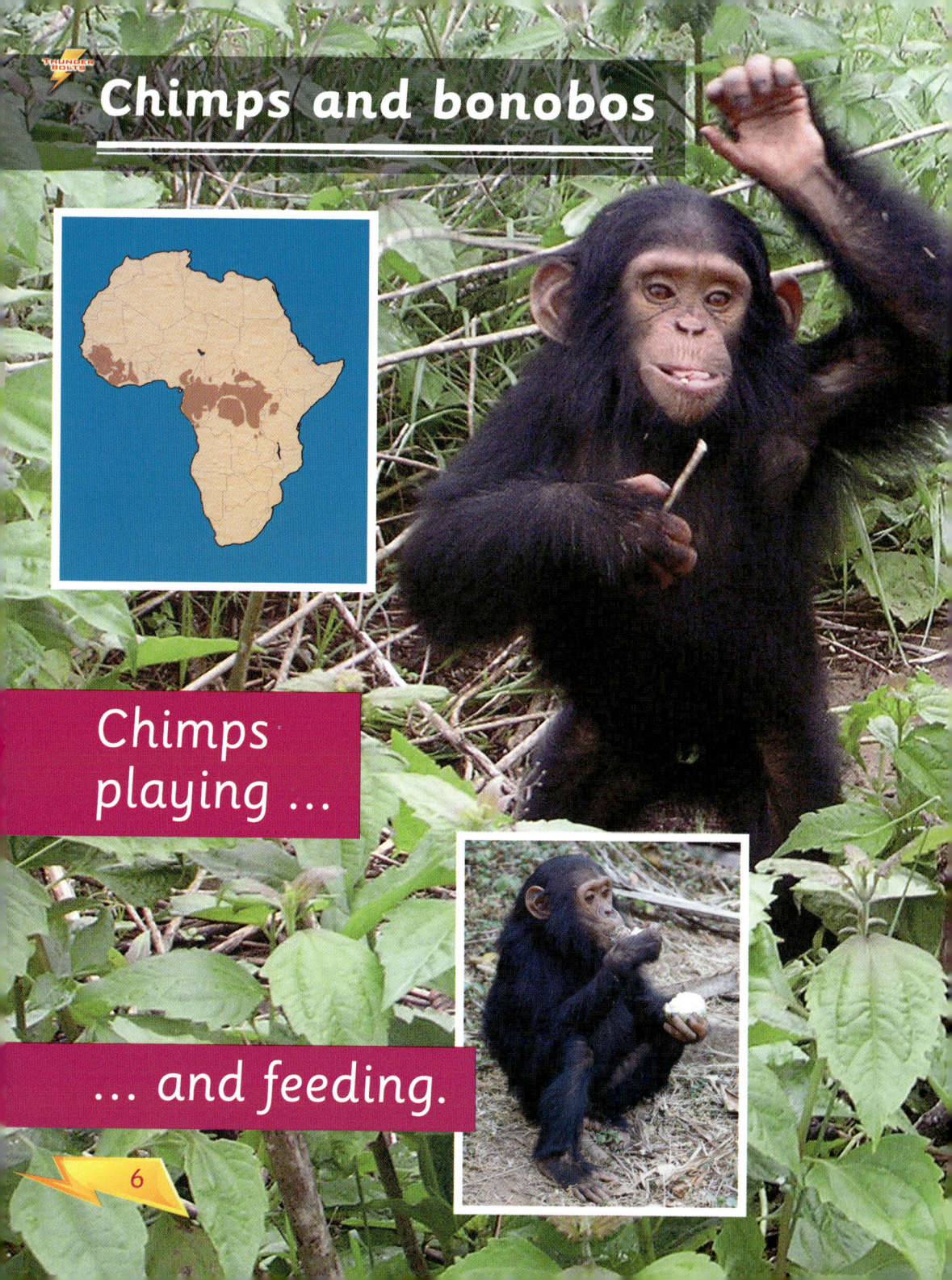

Chimps playing ...

... and feeding.

A bonobo.

Orang-utans

Orang-utans live mostly in trees.

Feeding.

Gorillas

Two silverback mountain gorillas.

Mother and baby.

Hunting for food.

What humans eat.

Using tools

A bonobo uses a stick to 'fish' for termites.

A gorilla uses a stick to get food.

Working together

A mother grooming her baby.

Apes in space!

This is Ham the chimp. He went into space in 1961.

This is Buzz Aldrin the human. He landed on the Moon in 1969.

Apes in trouble

Is it good to put animals in clothes?

What do you think?

Animals in cages

Many animals in zoos live in cages.

Should we keep animals in cages?

Should we keep animals in zoos?

The Burglars

That night ...

Word list

amazing
ape
baby
bonobo
burglar
chimp
clothes
feeding
gorilla
grooming
human
hungry
mother

mountain
orang-utan
silverback
space
termite
together